KABBALAH FOR BEGINNERS

An Introduction To The Wisdom Of Kabbalah

By Michele Gilbert

<u>Visit My Amazon Author Page</u>

Dedicated to those who choose to stretch beyond their own limits
and to seek a more abundant and fulfilling life.

Your thoughts are creative.

Michele Gilbert

My Free Gift To You!

As a way of saying thank you for downloading my book, I am willing to give you access to a selected group of readers who (every week or so) receive inspiring, life-changing kindle books at deep discounts, and sometimes even absolutely free.

Wouldn't it be great to get amazing Kindle offers delivered directly to your inbox?

Wouldn't it be great to be the first to know when I'm releasing new fresh and above all sharply discounted content?

But why would I so something like this?

Why would I offer my books at such a low price and even give them away for free when they took me countless hours to produce?

Simple.... because I want to spread the word!

For a few short days Amazon allows Kindle authors to promote their newly released books by offering them deeply discounted (up to 70% price discounts and even for free. This allows us to spread the word extremely quickly allowing users to download thousands and thousands of copies in a very short period of time.

Once the timeframe has passed, these books will revert back to their normal selling price. That's why you will benefit from being the first to know when they can be downloaded for free!

So are you ready to claim your weekly Kindle books?

You are just one click away! Follow the link below and sign up to start receiving awesome content

Thank you and Enjoy!

Table of contents

Introduction:

There was a point in the early 2000's where little red strings were tied around the wrists of a whole bunch of celebrities and that the word Kabbalah was being thrown around as vogue. It was everywhere and celebrities all over the country were excited about it and there really wasn't any explanation about it. In fact, if you run around and ask a bunch of people what it is that Kabbalah actually is, they're going to say that they have no idea what it is, except that people were wearing these funny little red strings around their wrists.

So, what is Kabbalah? What do they actually believe and where did it all come from? If you're part of the many people who are confused as to what Kabbalah is and how exactly it rolls in together, then this is the book that you're going to want to read.

In these pages, you're going to find a whole bunch of information that I can provide for you, whether it's just out of curiosity or whether you're going to look to make it a part of your life. So, let me break down exactly what you're getting yourself into. After all, everyone wants to know what it is that they're signing up for. So, take a look and see.

First up, I'm going to explain very briefly what it is that Kabbalah is and where it came from. It's quite an interesting tale as to where Kabbalah first appeared from on the scene and it's not exactly what a lot of people would expect, especially where it originates from.

Next up, I'm going to talk about some of the principle beliefs that are a part of Kabbalah and how they are viewed by practitioners of the faith in the context of their religion. It's a complex religion and there's a lot of it that goes deep down the rabbit hole of their faith, but I'm going to give you the bare bones of what you're looking for.

After that, I'm going to go into the tenants of the faith. These are going to be the principles and the beliefs that are foundational to their way of life and it's going to go a lot deeper into these principles so that you can really sink your teeth into some of the ideas that they're making a part of their life.

After that, I'm going to discuss some of the criticisms that Kabbalah faces and why it has taken a small role in the spotlight in the years that have passed. When it came into the vogue scene, it was attacked on multiple fronts and I think it's important that every religion that you're exploring you see the good and the bad. These are going to be the problems that several critics have found with the faith and why it has silently melted away recently.

So this is what you're going to get reading this book. It's going to be a fantastic ride and I'm so very excited to give you a glimpse at one of the most mysterious and intriguing religions that burst onto the scene and then silently faded back into the obscurity where it has existed for hundreds of years. So, without any more hesitating or discussion, let's have a look then.

The Brief Overview:

Asking what is Kabbalah is about as complex and confusing as asking what Christianity, Islam, Hinduism, or Buddhism is. It's a complex and vast system of belief that spreads across a whole ocean of theology that has been developed over the centuries. It is a confusing and strange system of belief that you're going to need a lot of background to understand completely, but right now, I'm going to give you the simplest and most refined interpretation of what Kabbalah is without going into too much detail as to what it means.

Essentially, when you ask a contemporary practitioner of Kabbalah what they are, they're going to be a person who practices an esoteric and mystical form of Judaism. Essentially, they're a faction or sect of the Jewish faith who have really broken off from the majority of the faith. While they see themselves as part of an almost radical or enlightened form of the Jewish faith, you will be hard pressed to find any Jewish figures that see Kabbalah as anything more than a misinformed, misguided, and delusional off shoot of Judaism. It's a harsh assessment, but when you see more of the aspects of Kabbalah, you're going to understand why it is so harshly looked upon by the Jewish community at large.

Kabbalists believe that their faith predates the existence of the Jewish structure of faith and was sort of hijacked by the Jewish faith for a long period of time. They believe that they are the root of primordial religious belief and that the Kabbalah beliefs are actually the foundation of the rest of the world religions. However, the truth of the matter is that they don't have any definitive existence until after the emergence of Jewish mystics in the middle ages. In fact, it's hard to find anything in a true form of Kabbalah before the emergences of the popular Hasidic Judaism in the 18th century. So, the declaration that it is a primordial belief isn't entirely accurate, but it is what they belief.

Essentially, what it is they belief is outlined as the understanding that there is a divine being known as Ein Sof who is what all other faiths describe as God and that humanity and creation must understand and reconcile their existence with this Ein Sof. One of their main texts is known as the Zohar and they believe that studying the Torah, the Christian Old Testament, is the foundation to finding the truth with Ein Sof. While there are four ways of interpreting the Torah, Kabbalah emphasizes the importance of the last, known as Sod, which is the inner, esoteric meanings of the Torah, which is secret knowledge and information. While most Jewish teachings find these Kabbalah ideas as heretical and untrue, Kabbalah believes that there is legitimacy to them and that they're the true teaching to find the truth of Ein Sof. In the end, they focus heavily on Jewish mystical literature that many Jews find to be little more than a distraction from true Jewish beliefs and have been abandoned.

Theoretical Kabbalah is the practice of seeking out a means to understand and to realize the divine realm that Ein Sof lives in and that we are all a part of. Then there is the introspection and communicative aspect known as Meditative Kabbalah where you seek to have a union with Ein Sof and understand what your relationship to him truly is. Finally there is Practical Kabbalah where you seek to alter the divine realm and the world. This is seen as magical thinking or white-magic as they describe it as. This is where the mystical aspect of Kabbalah really ramps up and revs into full gear.

Since Kabbalah is often seen as a rogue offshoot of Judaism, or the outlaw Judaism, it's really hard to nail down what it is that they believe. There are so many different interpretations and understanding of Kabbalah that you'll find a whole lot of people discussing different aspects of it with multiple focuses. While some seek to follow the Meditative communion of Kabbalah, or the academic Theoretical Kabbalah, the allure of Practical Kabbalah is definitely the more flashy and interesting to so many of them. Although all of these are basic schools of thought within them, there is one basic idea that Kabbalah pursues and that's the thought that there is mystic and mythic knowledge in the Torah that is not seen elsewhere in the world.

They believe that God revealed secrets to Adam and that there is a completely different account of Creation and God's first interactions with Adam and Eve as well as the interactions with the Serpent in the Garden of Eden. Not only do they have a different take on this, but they also have different understandings of the Tree of Knowledge of Good and Evil as well as the Tree of Life. Deeper in the Torah, they find more information that they believe is revealed to them in the prophetic visions of the various characters in the Bible, including Moses and the Burning Bush, Ezekiel's visions, Jacob's ladder to heaven, and Moses at Mount Sinai.

Ultimately, this secret knowledge is the foundation upon everyone practicing Kabbalah believes in. They are profoundly interested in forbidden, hidden, or lost knowledge that others have either discarded or ignored over the passage of time. So, if you want to dive into the mystical, mysterious, and forgotten aspects of the Jewish faith, then Kabbalah is more of an interesting search for those looking to find more of it. This is what you're looking for when you look into Kabbalah.

So, let's get a little more of the history as to where Kabbalah comes from in the history of the world. It'll give you a little more information as to what you're dealing with here. Without further adieu, I'll give you everything you need in a quick overview of a religion's history.

History of Kabbalah:

When it comes to the history of the Kabbalah faith, it's impossible to separate it from the faith of the Jewish people. The Jewish faith is one of the oldest and best documented theocracies and religious faiths in the history of the world and because of that, we have a long and extensive understanding of where the Jewish people came from and how they're perceived by culture around them.

The Jewish faith was established through the migration of man named Abraham who relocated from Mesopotamia and established himself in what is currently known as Israel and Palestine. After growing his family and building a culture, his people were reported to have been carried off into captivity in ancient Egypt. This is where the Torah begins, because while in Egypt, it is said that a central figure to their faith, Moses, wrote the Torah and the literature that the Jewish faith is built upon.

When the Jews were miraculously released form their captivity in Egypt, they journeyed across the Sinai desert and acquired mystical tablets known as the Ten Commandments and the Arc of the Covenant. Their conquest of Israel was mired with strange and miraculous events that built up this belief that there was a truly blessed and mysterious power around the Jewish people. Again, over and over, there were constant events throughout the Jewish history that would imply that there was something truly mystical and powerful at work in the Jewish community. This inevitably led to a lot of interest in the Jewish faith. This interest would mix and channel itself into a lot of hidden knowledge that people continually tried to keep to a minimum or keep a command over. Essentially, Judaism grew and was fostered in the midst of paganism, which was also extremely despised by the Jewish religious community. The enjoyment of esoteric ideas, mysticism, and magic was despised and hated by the normal community. However, it was still studied and explored by the Rabbis of the time.

The Maccabean Revolt is one of the high points in the history of the Jewish territory after the Jews were once again freed from captivity from the pagan

Babylonian Empire. After the Persian Empire freed the Jews from the Babylonians, Zoroastrianism, a religion steeped in mysticism, flooded the world. When Alexander the Great conquered the Persian Empire, taking over the Jewish territory of Israel and began to oppress the Jews. This led to the Maccabean Revolt, which was the birth of mysterious sects in the Jewish region. It was now that the esoteric ideals began to show up, a hunt for the mystical began to grow.

Judaism reached its apex at the height of their accomplishment when the Roman Empire was occupying their territory. At this point, the arrival of a mysterious prophet claiming to be the Jewish Christ appeared, called Jesus. With the explosion of Christianity also came the wrath of the Roman Empire who inevitably brought about many different sects of Judaism into a radical and violent force. This is something eventually lead to the complete destruction of the territory of Israel. In the end, it was time for the Jewish community to begin to spread and the Roman Empire was the perfect route for the Jewish people to spread their faith all across the world.

Now, so far, this has been the story of the Jewish people and not the faith of Kabbalah, but all of that changes with the expansion of the Muslim nations that took Israel in the name of Islam rather than Judaism or Christianity. Judaism spread all across Europe. It is here that Kabbalah breaks off of Judaism and actually begins to form its own presence. Of course, it wasn't known as Kabbalah at the time, but it was the beginning of the rise of Kabbalah.

While the Jews were constantly subjects of barbaric assaults from the Christian Kingdoms of Europe, they were also some of the most mysterious and confusing people in the religious world. It was often believed that the Jews were into mystical and magical arts that made a lot of people worried. Because of their constant oppression, the Jewish community started to look for more esoteric ideas in their faith. They also sought out the answers to the questions that were bothering them.

In southern France and in Spain, Jewish academics were taking great strides in uncovering the esoteric understandings and knowledge that the Jewish people had hidden away for a while. It was during this time that contemporaries state that Kabbalah underwent a massive historical reformation and was researched heavily by academics of the time. Of course, this is often disputed with many of the current Jewish scholars who believe that Kabbalah was little more than esoteric curiosity to disgruntled Jews of the time.

It wasn't until further developments in history came through the development of Spain who was heavily distraught throughout history by the Inquisition, the Reconquista, and the Islamic Invasion before all of it. This made Spain a hot bed of conflict, which also meant that the Jews were the least of the problems for the Christian Spaniards. This means that the esoteric beliefs of the Jews were easily explored and studied. Spain became the center of all Kabbalah research and understanding throughout the middle Ages until it began to resurge around the Renaissance. It was during this time that the Zohar, the Kabbalah religious text, began to make its appearance and grow in prominence.

Throughout history, Kabbalah study would rise and fall, depending upon the arrival of mystics upon the scene, but eventually, Kabbalah was banned in the 16th century for lacking accuracy and was known as heretical or blasphemous. Essentially, Jews at the time felt that there were a lot more pressing concerns than mysticism and that trying to understand heretical or secret knowledge wasn't that big of a deal. However, when the ban on studying Kabbalah was lifted, there was another surge in the renewed interested. Kabbalah began to grow and flourish again among the Jewish community looking for a sign of the Jewish Messiah to come and rescue the Jewish people who were suffering more and more with each passing year. In the end, there were two schools of Kabbalah at this time. The Kabbalah of the Sephardi in Spain and Portugal was popular in Europe, while the Kabbalah of the Mizrahi was popular in the Middle East, Africa, and Eastern Europe. Today, you will still find these two philosophies of Kabbalah in the world today.

Throughout the history of Kabbalah, several reformations and refinements have risen out of the Jewish community to lend credibility and interest to

Kabbalah, which tends to be disdained and hated among the contemporary scholars of the day. Even today, you will find that the majority of Jewish teachers will support Kabbalah to an extent of interest, but the dominant study of Kabbalah is very much close to Heresy.

It wasn't until the arrival of Kabbalah on the celebrity and public scene that Kabbalah was once more talked about in respected circles. Even today, Jews all across the world are plagued with tolerated persecution and social stigmas as to their beliefs. There are many in America who believe that Jewish societies are at the heart of everything from Hollywood to the Banks and in the government even. When Kabbalah exploded into the celebrity spotlight, it was once again criticized as being vogue for the elite of the world to be dabbling in Judaism. However, the mystical and divine ideas of Kabbalah have very little to do with the Jewish community as a whole.

Today, there is very little to link the Kabbalah societies and culture of the world to Judaism. In fact, you would be hard pressed to find a member of the Jewish community who actually acknowledges Kabbalah as a part of their faith outside of Talmudic study or an aspect of their faith. Beyond that, they will look upon practices of Kabbalah as a perversion of Judaism. Much like it could be said that Protestants are a perversion of Catholicism.

However, Kabbalah ahs been an acknowledged and even successful religion for quite some time now and it has made everything different in the lives of many of those that have found comfort and enlightenment in their teachings. It is those teachings that I want to go into next. There's so much that the Kabbalists of the world have been looking for answers since the Middle Ages and before. So, let's have a look at what it is they've learned about and see if any of it makes sense to you, whether it's a religion you'd be interested in looking into or not. Now, let's have a look at what it was that made them the mystery of the world.

Aspects of Kabbalah:

As far as the teachings of Kabbalah are concerned, there are some profound theological differences between Judaism and Kabbalah. Remember, there are also some distinct similarities that conjoin the two, so if things look familiar to you, there is an undeniable reason for that. However, it is important to stress that there was a clear and obvious rift between the two doctrines and you'll no doubt enjoy seeing what makes Kabbalah so unique. Now, without any further adieu, let's see what it is that makes Kabbalah such a fascinating, complex, and controversial religion of the world.

God Revealed and Concealed:

Kabbalah teaches that there are two aspects to God that have to be reconciled to us and that we understand. Ein Sof, as they call God, has an essence that is absolute in its transcendence and is limitless as well as unknowable. After all, a divine being is beyond our understanding and this divine being would also be beyond our comprehension if we tried to understand the motivations and the truths that God had for us. This is known as the Concealed God and that puts us at a severe disadvantage as humans in the service of God. We cannot possibly know, understand, or anticipate what it is God will do, why he does it, or how we truly play into his divine plan.

However, there is an alternative to that, another side to the coin, as you might find helpful in understanding. But, there is also a manifestation of God, which is revealed to all of us through this persona that we perceive as God. To understand and perceive what it is that this God wants through the creation that is all around us. How God interacts with the world is yet another way that we can perceive and understand this Revealed God, but it is through these actions that we realize what it is that the Revealed God wants. However, we must also remember that this Revealed God is the perception that he wants us to see and that we need to understand that this revealed aspect of God speaks volumes to his intentions and motivations as well.

It is in this Concealed God that so much of Kabbalah finds its interest and its fascination, while the majority of Judaism spends its time studying the Revealed God that they also acknowledge. The legitimacy of this Concealed God and what they want to discover and discern is always in questions which makes Kabbalists constantly question, search, and hunger for information.

So, at the core of any faith is the interpretation and understanding of the ultimate authority in the universe. For Kabbalah it is a God that both hides and shows his face to his children and it is how he shows his face that makes us the most curious about him. The idea of a dualistic creator with a definite plan for how he interacts with his creation makes this God seem almost intimidating at first and impossible to truly know. That puts us at a disadvantage, but Kabbalah takes comfort in this nature of God and explains it further.

The Ten Sefirot:

When it comes to understanding both the Concealed God and the Revealed God, both are manifested in ten attributes that are called the Sefirot. Each of these ten attributes are used to describe what it is God wants from his people and what it is that he does to reveal himself through creation, his actions, and the way he speaks to us through prophetic teaching. Each of these attributes are vital to the understanding and the ability to understand God and the secret mysteries and mystical power that he has for all of us.

The Sefirot are most easily understood and explained in Kabbalah by pulling an analogy between the Tree of Life and several other mysterious analogies that the Kabbalah has. When you look up Kabbalah, you're bound to find an image of ten circles that look like a tree, this is the explanation of the Sefirot and a tool for explaining it all to them.

I'm going to invest some time in each of these ten attributes, since they're vital to the understanding of God and how the Kabbalists operate with spiritual matters. So, let's have a look at them so we can understand them better.

Keter:

Keter is also known as the Crown and the reason for this is the simple fact that a crown is worn above the head. So in essence, Keter is an explanation of everything that is above the mind that cannot be comprehended. This is everything that is above us. This is the essence of the Concealed God and the fact that there is more out there that we will never have the answer to. This is the abstract kind of ideals that we are not able to touch, hold, or truly express without help. This is the primal stirrings that are presented to us that we claw at without really being able to understand it. Since Ketere is the first on the list, it is also the most divine and the highest of all of them.

Chokhmah:

Chokhmah is also known as the wisdom and this is the first power of conscious intelligence within Creation as a whole and is the first point of a real existence. This is most commonly associated with the right eye or the right hemisphere of the brain. If you can fully enhance and encourage this ability then Chokham possesses two faces. The first is Abba lla'ah, known as the Higher Father and the lower is Yisrael Saba, known as the Elder. In the end this is pushing for your ability to look deeply at aspects of reality and abstract concepts until you can truly discern the axiomatic truth. This is the primary force of the creative process because you need wisdom and understanding of the truth of something before you can fully unleash something.

Binah:

Alternative to Chokhmah is Binah, which is associated with the left eye and the left side of the brain. Binah is known as something a little more complex, such as the understanding of the potential in something. This is your intuition that speaks to you and your ability to contemplate something. It is the ability to reflect upon truth once it is discovered and tear apart Creation to find out what it truly means. From Chokhmah, Binah amplifies and digests what wisdom is learned and what truths can be found in the world. It is our ability to process and develop the wisdom that we've been shown into something a bit more substantial and powerful than we've originally thought. It is also associated with the feminine aspects of the world, including women. When one has fully developed Binah, it also has two aspects of its existence. Imma ila'ah, known as the Higher Mother and then the lower which is known as tevunah, which is known as comprehension. Both of these form Imma, which is known as the mother.

Da'at:

Beneath and between Chokhmah and Binah is Da'at, which is sometimes referred to as an empty slot or otherwise identified as an expansion and reflection of the wisdom and understanding that comes from the previous two. This is something that you're going to really want to know as more of an amplification through the intellectual process. There's something about Da'at that isn't singularly a sefirot, but actually a unification of all of them. This is everything firing on full power and every cylinder is charging at full power. This is the power to balance everything that is making this higher power something of an intellectual weapon. All of it is working in harmony and unison. Without Da'at, everything falls apart and everything is out of balance. A person is very interested in having Da'at in their life to make sure that everything is working in unity.

Chesed:

When it comes to Chesed, it is most often translated as something close to loving-kindness, kindness, or love. Rather than coming up with an intellectual aspect, Chesed is more of an ethical and theological term that is utilized for the compassionate side of the world. It is a valued aspect of every Jewish denomination, not just Kabbalah and is an attribute that is required by all denominations for the repairing of the world around us. It is through Chesed that all of Creation will be healed, fixed, and brought back. This is the first emotive attribute of the sefirot when it comes to the Kabbalah. They ask that you love God so completely that you will never turn your back on Him. They ask that you provide for children with anything that they could ever need and to do it with love. It also heavily emphasizes the visiting and healing of the sick, tending to the poor, and giving hospitality to the strangers of the world. There is also a heavy push for you to attend to the dead and there is also a demand to keep the peace between the people of the world. This is the faith of God in action.

Gevurah:

This is the second emotive attribute of the sefirot and Gevurah is also the essence of judgment and limitation. It is the ability that corresponds to awe and the element of fire. This is the righteous attribute that demands that there is change in the world to right the wrongs that have been inflicted upon the world. This is God's mode of punishing the wrongdoers and the wicked of the world. This is God's wrath and divine intervention in the form of his punishment. This is the strict adherence to the law and the absolute matter of justice. This is the other side of Chesed, this is the action that is required and demanded by divine law. It is said that Gevurah is your ability to hold back your primal desire to do good on another when they are unworthy of it and require punishment. This is your ability to configure the world in the right image of God and to right the wrongs that plague it.

Tiferet:

Tiferet is the ability to the compassion of Chesed and the strength of Gevurah together and to reconcile them together. At this point, these two forces are giving and receiving. In the end, this is the power of mercy. This is how loving compassion restrains the demand for justice and punishment. This is our ability to work with both of them. It is part of the middle pillar of the Tree of Life, which means that it is the ability to bring together two traits and to spread it out among the others. It reminds us that justice and punishment must be in balance with love and compassion. One cannot outweigh the other and we must work with them in unison, rather than being dominant with another. Without Tiferet, your ability to keep your emotive powers in check is going to be nearly impossible to maintain. Having it is required to understand the Concealed and Revealed God.

Netzach:

Netzach is translated into eternity and is the perpetuity, victory, and endurance of God that the Kabbalah demands to be acknowledged. This is the first that we're going to discuss that is known as the tactical sefirot. In the meaning of tactical, it speaks to its acquisition of something else. This tells us what is happening in the world around you, you don't look at things with face value but rather as the means to the end that they lead to. This is a sefirot that is focused on man and what is most appropriate way for man to receive God's knowledge. This is the endurance and fortitude to follow through with your passion to the ends that you meet. This is the leadership and ability to rally those that are going to help you with the cause and motivate them to act in the best interest of God's plan.

Hod:

Hod is translated as majesty, splendor, and glory. It is the means for you to have activity and to accomplish your goals. Hod is often compared to your feet, where as hands accomplish tasks, Hod is what brings your to those tasks. Hod is your ability to subdue your problems and over come them. It is where form is given to language and is the key to the mystery of form. It's what's going to get you to accomplish your goals and to get things done.

Yesod:

Yesod is known as foundation and it is your ability to understand what it is that you're doing. When it comes to Yesod, it's your foundation, your understanding and your knowledge. It's not just your spiritual presence, but the community with which you work. As you look around at the foundation of the world that you're in, it's going to give you the power to change that world. Think of foundation as the world all around you and the actual presence of Creation in your life. This is what's going to be changed around you. This is what you're working to change in the world around you, to heal, and save.

Malkuth:

This is the bottom of the Tree of Life and it is the last of the Sefirot, which means that it is the last part that we'll be talking about. Malkuth is what is known as the spiritual kingdom of God and this is the final victory that everything is working toward. This is the bridegroom of God and it's the ultimate goal of everyone to bring the spiritual kingdom to eminence in the world. This is going to do everything in the world and it is going to be the force that changes everything. In the end, this is the seed of everything that is going to grow out of this movement.

Evil and the Role of Man:

Evil is seen as a necessary aspect of the world around you. It is what's going to be at conflict with everything that you're trying to do when you're in the Kabbalah. Evil is not seen as a malevolent force, but as soemthign that is required for God to exist. If it were not for evil and conflict in the world, then God would have no comparison to anything else. Without the evil of the world, we would not recognize the goodness of God and the desire that is to be with him and have communion with God. So, if evil is a force that is necessary, then it is our job to make sure that we do everything in our power to ensure that we understand that evil will always exist and that there will always be perceived evils out there.

What isn't evil that is sanctioned by God is the evils that are created by man. As part of Creation, it is our job to be reconciled to God, to understand everything that we can about him, and that we work our hardest to become close to God.

Since that's not in everyone's toolkit, we're also subject to righting the wrongs that man inflicts upon their fellow man. So, according to Kabbalah, it is our job to make sure that we're reconciled to God and that we are actively searching for what we can possibly know about God.

Reincarnation:

The transmigration of the soul is something that is very popular in the Kabbalah circle of the world. It is called Gilgul neshamot or the Cycles of the soul. It is a concept that isn't extremely promoted in Judaism any longer, but it is something that Kabbalists have latched onto for a long time now. It is a literary motif and it's something that many in Kabbalah are extremely intrigued by.

There are hundreds of aspects of Kabbalah that you're going to find very intriguing and interesting and all of these are just the beginning. There is a whole lot of mysticism inside Kabbalah that is held in the Zohar and in the other texts that they are intrigued by. The deeper you look into Kabbalah, the more you're going to notice that it's something that is extremely complex and very deep. So, if these have intrigued you, then I hope that you'll continue looking deeper and deeper into the subject material.

Conclusion:

When it comes to Kabbalah, it's an interesting world that is full of mystery and even more confusion than most religions. Since it popped into the spotlight years ago and then simultaneously vanished, you'll notice that this is a cyclical pattern that Kabbalah has been going up and down throughout history. It's something that you're going to come to expect when it comes to Kabbalah, but it's never down for long. The mystical aspects of Judaism tends to make things interesting in the religious community and there's a lot of rich and historical material to pull through.

However, Judaism has often attacked Kabbalah because there is something that makes religious communities angry when heretical material and singular aspects of the faith are exploited for public appeal, however, some say this anger is unfounded. Some say that Kabbalists are simply dedicated to a single aspect of Judaism that many see as out of balance to others. It is constantly under attack and others are constantly scrutinizing it in the Jewish community. While there is always going to be a lot of eyes watching Kabbalah, it's still going to probe for the answers to the questions that plague us in the spiritual community and world.

Regardless of how it is viewed, Kabbalah is here to stay and it's been here for a long time. If you've found something in this book that has whet your appetite for more information on it, I hope that you find it. It's important for us to continue to understand and discover more about other religions in the world. If you liked exploring this topic, I hope that you can find more information delving into the rich history and heritage of this faith.

Before you go, I'd like to say thank you for purchasing my book.

I know you could have picked so many other books to read on better sleep.

But you took a chance on me.

So A Big thanks for downloading this book and reading it all the way to completion.

Now I would like to ask a _small_ favor.

Could you please take a minute or two to leave a review for this book on Amazon?

Click here

The feedback will help me continue to publish more kindle books that will help people to get better results in their lives.

And if you found it helpful in anyway then please let me know :-)

Thank you and good luck!

To your success,

Michele

Preview of My New Book

<u>Listening Skills: Master The Art Of Listening And Communication Skills For A More Confident Life</u>

CHAPTER ONE

Have you ever heard someone repeat the old saying that religious people have been using since someone drifted off while they were speaking? God only gave us one mouth and two ears so that we would listen twice as much. Well, I'm not an overly religious person and I'm not sure that I have the answers to the Cosmos or the greater questions in life, but I do have a response to that. It's pretty much true, in a sense.

If there is one thing that can drive a man or woman insane is the scenario that no one will listen to them. Ever want to communicate something only to have someone completely miss what you're saying? It's enough to make your hands clench into a fist and your blood boil. There's a reason for this.

There are many who believe that the greatest desire of the human being is to be understood and the key to being understood is communication. Communication brings us together, binds us, inspires us, educates us, enlightens us, and relaxes us. It's the way intimacy is built and it's the way validation is given. Without communication, we are entirely isolated in a world that we don't entirely understand and that can be stifling and terrifying to man. But the key to communication is that there are three aspects to it. They are thought, vocalization, and interpretation. One is the art of the mind and how to think of things. The second is the art of the mouth and how to coin those thoughts into a medium by which we can share or test these thoughts. But for us, the focus is the art of the ear, receiving the words of others so that they might inspire our minds or that we might help them.

While we spend copious amounts of time shackled to our minds and often feel the urge to spread our ideas, thoughts, or questions; we are very diligent in neglecting the art of the ear. Our ability to truly listen and understand others is very hard, because it's something we don't always want to utilize and that becomes a problem. If you don't listen to your friends, your coworkers, or your wife; then you're destined for failure in your relationships.

That's why the art of the ear is vital for you to understand if you want to boost your relationships. So here's the rub for you. If you want to energize, invigorate your relationships, then you're going to want to take this book and study it closely because there is one thing that I can promise you. The more you utilize your ears, the more you will inspire and influence those around you to keep coming back. Those who listen more than they talk give off the aura of wisdom, intelligence, and more than that, it isn't a lie. It isn't wrong. Do you understand that? People who listen more than they talk are wise and they are intelligent. Because in the end, you'll understand that there is more to the world that you can learn by listening and the more you learn the smarter you are and the wiser you'll become.

If you want to be a sage person and to experience life without actually having to go through the suffering and the pain of hurts and wrongs; then start listening. People will be inspired by you, they will come to you, and they will invest their lives with you if they know that you're willing to truly listen to them. This is something that you're bound to find out if you just take the time to study the art of the ear.

So whether you want to inspire your coworkers, influence those around you, or find that deeper level of intimacy with your spouse, then take notes, keep an open mind, and start utilizing the things you learn here the moment you put this book down. I guarantee that you'll start seeing the difference immediately in those around you.

CHAPTER TWO

The Ballad of the Man Who Wouldn't Listen

Now we all know someone in their life that wouldn't actually listen to them, but more importantly, we all know someone who has screwed up their life royally by not listening. Sooner or later, there's a person who gets their life completely into the dumps, sucked down in the muck until there's nothing that can really save them all because when it boils down to it, it comes down to not listening.

<u>**Click here to read the rest of**</u>
<u>**Listening skills**</u>

P.S. You'll find many more books like this and others under my name Michele Gilbert.

Don't miss them... here is a short list.

<u>**Stop Playing Mind Games: How To Free Yourself Of Controlling And Manipulating Relationships**</u>

<u>**Instant Charisma: A Quick And Easy Guide To Talk, Impress, And Make Anyone Like You**</u>

<u>**Chakras: Understanding The 7 Main Chakras For Beginners: The Ultimate Guide To Chakra Mindfulness, Balance and Healing**</u>

<u>**Practicing Mindfulness: Living in the moment through Meditation: Everyday Habits and Rituals to help you achieve inner peace**</u>

<u>**Introduction To Palmistry: The Ultimate Palm Reading Guide For Beginners**</u>

<u>**Emotional Intelligence: How to Succeed By Mastering Your Emotions And Raising Your IQ**</u>

<u>**Wicca: The Ultimate Beginners Guide For Witches and Warlocks: Learn Wicca Magic**</u>

<u>**The Introvert's Advantage: The Introverts Guide To Succeeding In An Extrovert World**</u>

<u>**Adrenal Fatigue: What Is Adrenal Fatigue Syndrome And How To Reset Your Diet And Your Life**</u>

<u>**Body Language 101: What A Person's Body Language Is Really Telling You...And How You Can Use It To Your Advantage**</u>

The Arthritis Pain Cure: How to find Arthritis Pain Relief and live a happy pain free life!

The Headache Pain Cure: How to find Headache Pain Relief and live a happy Pain Free Life!

Stop Panic Attacks and Anxiety Disorders without Drugs Now!: Overcome Panic, Stress and Anxiety and live a happy pain free life!

The Breakup Recovery Guide: Advice for Surviving Heartbreak, Letting Go and Thriving in an exciting new life!

The Friendship Guide to Finding Friends Forever: How to Find, Make and Keep Quality Friendships After your Breakup

The Credit Fix: Leave behind credit card debt and poor credit scores and get your life back!

How To Stop Being Jealous And Insecure: Overcome Insecurity And Relationship Jealousy

The Breakup Recovery Guide: Advice for Surviving Heartbreak, Letting Go and Thriving in an exciting new life!

The Friendship Guide to Finding Friends Forever: How to Find, Make and Keep Quality Friendships After your Breakup

The Credit Fix: Leave behind credit card debt and poor credit scores and get your life back!

How To Stop Being Jealous And Insecure: Overcome Insecurity And Relationship Jealousy

My Free Gift To You!

As a way of saying thank you for downloading my book, I am willing to give you access to a selected group of readers who (every week or so) receive inspiring, life-changing kindle books at deep discounts, and sometimes even absolutely free.

Wouldn't it be great to get amazing Kindle offers delivered directly to your inbox?

Wouldn't it be great to be the first to know when I'm releasing new fresh and above all sharply discounted content?

But why would I so something like this?

Why would I offer my books at such a low price and even give them away for free when they took me countless hours to produce?

Simple.... because I want to spread the word.!

For a few short days Amazon allows Kindle authors to promote their newly released books by offering them deeply discounted (up to 70% price discounts and even for free. This allows us to spread the word extremely quickly allowing users to download thousands and thousands of copies in a very short period of time.

Once the timeframe has passed, these books will revert back to their normal selling price. That's why you will benefit from being the first to know when they can be downloaded for free!

So are you ready to claim your weekly Kindle books?

You are just one click away! Follow the link below and sign up to start receiving awesome content

Thank you and Enjoy!

About Michele

Michele Gilbert was born and raised in Brooklyn, New York. Drawn to literature and writing at a young age, she enrolled at Brooklyn College and majored in English. After graduation Michele did not begin writing immediately, instead she embarked on a career in the finance industry and spent the next thirty years on Wall Street.

Serendipity struck when she least expected it. After ending a long-term relationship, Michele found herself lost and unsure what the future held. She began to read books on grief and loss, looking for answers. Those led her to delve deeper into the Law of Attraction and its power. What resulted was remarkable. Not only had she begun to heal, she had also rekindled her former love of writing and discovered her life's purpose.

The years have taken her through many twists and turns, but she learned valuable lessons along the way. Today she publishes books-mostly self-help and metaphysical in nature-and feels compelled to share her knowledge with those facing similar experiences. Her greatest hope is to inspire others and show them ways to overcome adversity and gracefully accept life's inevitable low points.

Going forward, she plans to incorporate more teachings of self-help, finance and meditation. Regular meditation is very beneficial to her progress as she forges a new life. Morning rituals and positive incantations are other practices Michele embraces; they are very restorative in daily life.

As an avid hiker, Michele and fellow club members often hike the picturesque Jersey Pine Barrens. She is a history buff, voracious reader, baseball fanatic and a foodie. She also proudly supports Trout Unlimited-a national non-profit organization dedicated to conserving, protecting and restoring North America's Coldwater fisheries and their watersheds.

Michele currently resides forty minutes from Atlantic City and the Jersey Shore. She makes her home with a Blue Russian rescue cat named Jersey, though she isn't exactly sure who rescued who.

Michele really enjoys publishing books that can make a difference in people's lives. If you have any suggestions or would like to have a specific topic covered in a future book, please send an email to michelegilbertbooks@gmail.com and we will get back to you.

Thanks for reading!

Made in the USA
Lexington, KY
22 August 2016